Tower of Lies

David Stant * Kaitlin Shearer

To my loving family and friends, who always have my back. And to everyone who has supported me along the way...........

Table of Contents

Part 1

Essays
Tower of Lies
America's Open Casket
Written by Kaitlin Shearer

I wrote the poem, Tower of Lies, and I put a lot of inner thoughts and opinions into it. I feel that our economy and our communities depend on the power of word of mouth. There are so many lies out there. There is no person who has never lied, and we as a country are based on these lies. When one person speaks truth, they are accused of lying or are told they are not worth anything. If there is a person who is kind, truthful,and decent, this world will beat them up over and over again. This poem shines some light on this. If we just open up a little bit, even baby steps, so many things would change for the better. I know its hard to change if you are holding on to the past, but we as a collective can let go together.

We must unmask our deceptions and move on as one people. The poem brings light to the fact that we as a people need to start working together and pushing past our fears of change. If we don't start now, it will be too late. Our economy is fragile. We are hurting others to make sure its still the same lies, still the same lies it has always been. Things won't be equal until we make them that way. We can make steps toward it. All we have to do is try, so I ask you to try something new to help someone. Try to make steps toward equality, steps to strengthen the earth before it is too late.

I wrote the poem, America's Open Casket, to explain that anyone can have hope, faith, or kindness. However, most people don't even try to grasp it. Instead, we wait for someone else to do it for us or for it to come to us. You can't be heard if you don't make noise. If you don't take action to obtain your freedom, you will never have it. This is what the poem is trying to get through to the reader in the first stanza. In the second stanza, the poem is describing how most people sit and watch good things pass because they are either too lazy, too tired, or feel they don't need these things. We mourn the loss of what could have been ours. It wasn't because we couldn't push ourselves to get it. We are giving away our freedom small piece by small piece, and most people don't even realize.

In conclusion, shoot your shot if you have an opportunity for something good coming your way. Get up, reach out, and take it. In the worst case scenario, you shoot your shot and fall down. I know it might sound scary, but all you have to do is lean on your family and friends. Then stand back up, and try again. "If at first you don't succeed, try try again"- William Edward Hickson.

Tower of Lies
Written by Kaitlin Shearer

Our world,

Our world you say?

Our world is a tower of lies,

Stacked on top of one another,

Until someone tries to stop them,

And they all come crashing down from the sky,

And its not alright, its not okay,

Not what just anyone else would say,

Because its not okay

We need to fix it

We need to fix it fast

Or our fragile earth won't last

America's Open Casket
Written by Kaitlin Shearer

Hope is everywhere,

Still most cannot grasp it,

Instead we all lie here,

In "America's Open Casket"

For all to see,

To mourn our loss,

The feeling of chills,

From a damp winter's frost

For all to see,

What once was free

Part 2

Essays
Lincoln's Bedside
Everlasting Union
Written by Kaitlin Shearer

The poems you are about to read are written by David Stant. Lincoln's Bedside is taking place after Lincoln was assassinated. The poem begins with Lincoln slowly slipping away and dying as he did in the history books. The same as in history he did not die immediately. This is when the poem is set. The poem considers how Lincoln and the United States would have moved forward if in fact Lincoln actually recovered. It touches on how the country and the world may have progressed differently.

In the beginning of the poem, however, David Stant does make it seem as though this false history was the true history in which Lincoln did not overcome this treachery. The lines, "by his bedside sadness becomes longing, desperation becomes a tormenting rage", touch on the true events in our nation's history. In the final announcement, the reader finds out that Lincoln has survived. This surprise ending offers a glimpse of how our country may have taken shape following the civil war had Lincoln not been assassinated.

The poem, Everlasting Union, goes further into detail about how people in the United States would have reacted to Lincoln's recovery.   The poem states, "A beam of light touches the ground at sunrise, decorates morning's dew with gold". These lines are referring to the day after Lincoln was shot. The poem goes on to state, "Hidden in the comforting safety, of a place far away from wars". This is telling the reader what would have happened had Lincoln survived. The country would not have been angry, sad, and most of all devastated, but instead peaceful.

At the end of the poem, the author states something that clues the reader in. The author wrote the last stanza based on the true history that Lincoln did actually die. In both poems, there are competing story lines, Lincoln Survives, Lincoln does not survive. In the poem, Everlasting Union, the reverse of Lincoln's Bedside takes place, finishing the combination of both poems with one man's possible reaction to Lincoln's death. The last stanza tells the reader that when Lincoln died so did many people's hopes of any sort of everlasting union.

These are both amazing poems, and I think you will enjoy reading them. I hope this background knowledge and insight from the author was helpful to your understanding of these two poems.

Lincoln's Bedside
Written by David Stant

Lincoln slips into infinite darkness

He lay expressionless, emotionless, skin colored pale white

A vision of the future hangs unequivocally in the balance

By his bedside, sadness becomes longing

By his bedside, desperation becomes a tormenting rage

The nation, expecting everlasting defeat,

Looks upon the coming announcement with despair

"Lincoln, to whom a dream has fostered change,

Recovers in the company of his beloved wife,

May we all bear forth our strongest convictions in the equality of men"

Everlasting Union
Written by David Stant

A beam of light touches the ground at sunrise

Decorates morning's dew with gold

Holding gracefully the mind of kind soul

That walks where justice meets truth

Hidden in the comforting safety

Of a place far away from wars

Lies a story not yet told

Being written in his illuminated consciousness

He walks a path within his mind

A pace, a yard, then ten

To where the grassy knoll first meets the trees

Then buries himself in his thoughts

"A nation divided cannot stand

And only in justice is this story told

But the hope of everlasting union

Died with the symbol of the cause"

Part 3

Essays
Hell's Gate
The Wind Blows
Written by Kaitlin Shearer

Hell's Gate is a poem I wrote. I wrote this poem while learning about the Holocaust. I am one fourth Jewish and would be in a concentration camp if I was alive then. That news shocked me. To think about how frightened or tired I would have gotten, or even my chances of survival at all, chills me to the bone. I have a very good teacher that delicately brought awareness of this event to our classroom environment.

The meaning behind the poem is simple. The holocaust was a truly devastating event. I wrote about all of the poor souls whose lives were unfairly taken from them. I wanted to bring awareness to the fact that if we are not careful this could happen again. Unfortunately, if we don't keep this devastating memory alive, history could repeat itself. As my teacher has said, "people are people, just with better toys". With this she means we tend to make the same mistakes, and I don't want to see that happen.

In the poem "Hell's Gate", I am reflecting on how fearful and afraid I think any person would have felt in this position. I feel that so many people began to realize that there was no hope. I can't imagine getting separated from your father or mother because of gender. I don't know what I would do without my father or other family members, anyone close to me just gone, and I left alone floating in never ending abyss.

I am haunted by the thought of babies being thrown into fires because they were of no use to the Nazi regime. Young children were being deprived of their childhood to instead get experimented on. Folks that looked or acted too old were burnt alive because they couldn't keep up with the outrageous workload.

The poem, "The Wind Blows", is about people losing hope. Imagine the situation that these people faced. Would you still have hope for you and your family? This poem vividly shows people losing all hope for a better, more peaceful fate. In the second stanza, the poem states, "encompasses the timelessness of waiting, left to the brutality of chance". Much like in a dream, their lives hung in the balance. They were at the mercy of their captors in the same manner as in a dream we are entirely at the mercy of our minds.

It is a legend that if you fall to earth in a dream, you die in your sleep. The subject in the poem is wishing the wind "will carry their fears to safety", a metaphor for escaping this horrible fate. This part of the poem is referring to when Americans joined the war and started liberating many concentration camps across Germany, freeing the people who had not yet had their lives stolen from them. Thus, the poem ends with their hopes of leading a life free of torture and murder "renewed".

Hell's Gate
Written by Kaitlin Shearer

If you were lucky, you might escape

If not, you had a frightening fate

If you were to go beyond hell's gate,

You would be afraid

If you've ever had an emotional scar,

If dreams were still too far,

If you were taken because of David's Star,

You would be afraid

If you've only heard, you don't quite know,

The dangers lurking in those camps below,

Keep passing on the truth, so,

The future isn't afraid

So the past won't repeat,

So he will face his final defeat,

I say these words with truth,

You would be afraid

The Wind Blows
Written by David Stant

A star moves across sky's black landscape

A beacon of light in a kingdom of darkness

As sudden as the star begins to soar

Light calls me within a dream to make a wish

A cool breeze begins to blow

Encompasses the timelessness of waiting

Left to the brutality of chance

When the star nears earth

I wish the wind

Will carry my fears to safety

Within its soft, subtle embrace

Part 4

Essays
A World Divided
Southern Tendency
Written by David Stant

The poem, A World Divided, focuses on a young African American woman living during the time of segregation. The first several lines of the poem, "she felt discarded.......stripping her of her pride", describe the emotionally devastating experience of being a second class citizen, looked down upon and discriminated against. The poem takes a turn when the subject realizes that she must begin to challenge the existing social order. Her memories of childhood enter her consciousness as she realizes that her experience has been unfair and cruel. The subject must first tackle this personal obstacle before taking a stand for her human rights. The subject in this case is a pioneer, waiting on the consciousness of the nation to change. The last two lines of the poem imply that this has not yet happened in her time.

It is interesting to look back upon this earlier period in our nation's history. Yet, as we have witnessed in modern politics, not as much as I was led to believe has changed. There is still a large part of our nation's population that feels the same as the subject's oppressors during the time of segregation. Hence, I have followed the poem, A World Divided, with the poem, Southern Tendency.

The poem, Southern Tendency, focuses on the experience of many young African Americans living in the South in present day. Too often those who are discriminated against are falsely led to believe that there voice is the same as the voice of their more privileged white peers. What ends up happening is their privileged white peers begin to speak for them, and little can be accomplished in the modern effort to fight racism and oppression. African Americans begin to rely on their white peers, thus developing a dependency on those who are actually discriminating against them. I finish this short poem with the line, "perhaps mankind's greatest felony", with the intent of highlighting the almost criminal nature of this all too common set of events.

A World Divided
Written by Kaitlin Shearer

She felt discarded,

Thrown away like the thousands of others,

The endless cycle of evil,

Depriving her of her spirit,

Stripping her of her pride

"Who decided the color of our skin will determine our legacy?"

Memories of childhood come flooding back,

She had now accepted the challenging fact,

But when would everyone else?

Until then we live,

A world divided

Southern Tendency
Written by David Stant

The moonlight cries upon a southern tendency

A young mind found too soon a dependency

Silent notes construct this melody

Perhaps mankind's greatest felony

Part 5

Essays
Beauty Queen
These Four Walls
Written By David Stant

Woman's rights are at the forefront of many of the social issues of our time, and "Beauty Queen" captures the pressure placed upon women to live up to unrealistic beauty standards. What the poem does exceptionally well is demonstrate, that by trying to live up to these standards, women experience an inner death. The last line of the poem, "painfully slips away", hones the reader in on the process of drowning in the subject's own ideas of perfection, which in this case, although not in every case, takes over the subject of the poem.

When at the age of the subject, there was much consideration given to the drop in self esteem women experience when young men begin to evaluate them based primarily on appearance. Many attempts have been made to empower young women to overcome this obstacle. However, the poem is describing an adolescent woman in the present tense, so one can infer that very little has changed. What new strategies can women deploy to improve upon the change in confidence and self judgment may well be a topic of discussion for years to come.

The subject of the poem is experiencing a symbolic death, and as the poem unfolds, one can begin to see how deeply troubling the issue of beauty standards appears to be. The word "bleeding" in the poem appears to mean that the desire to enjoy life is leaving the subject through a wound that oppressive culture has created. The metaphorical would is located on the subject's stomach, one of the likely imperfections that a man would place unequal judgment upon. The subject of the poem does come to a realization that her desire for physical perfection has left her feeling empty, though the subject of the poem is still placing judgment upon herself while having this realization.

A connection can be made in the poem, "These Four Walls", between the first and third stanzas, where the way the room is decorated is creating an "aha" moment for the subject. I realize in this moment that my mother only wanted to protect me, despite the many difficulties our relationship has presented.

In the middle stanza, a delicate ceramic piece is protecting "coffee", my only lasting romance, from damaging the mahogany table, the center of the room's attention. The scene is a metaphor for the delicate way in which my mother protected me from a long term relationship I was in with an addict who was struggling to stay clean. Throughout life, I was always the center of my mother's attention.

In relation to "Beauty Queen", the realization that one's mother only wants to protect them could offer comfort and peace amid the harsh realities of any number of circumstances. In the case of "Beauty Queen", this realization could potentially save the subject from drowning in her own ideas of perfection. "These Four Walls" is meant to be a poem serving as the light at the end of the tunnel for the subject of "Beauty Queen".

Beauty Queen
Written by Kaitlin Shearer

She is a beauty queen,

A slave to society's vision of beautiful,

Drowning slowly in a bottomless pit of make-up and high heels

It took her years to realize,

It will take her life from her, kill her

She looks at her stomach, bleeding

She thinks of the meaningless things,

Of how she has wasted her life,

She is scared to reveal her true self

At what cost? The beauty queen painfully slips away

These Four Walls
Written by David Stant

These four walls, colored cream,

With paintings of flowers evenly spaced

A cup of coffee rests gracefully

On a mahogany table

An antique porcelain trivet

Patterned royal blue and white

Saves my only lasting romance

From damaging the center

Of the room's captured attention

A question once a mystery

Presents a simple, hidden answer

That my dear, loving mother

Wanted only to protect her child

Part 6

Essays
Silver Dagger
A Blooming Friendship
Written By David Stant

"Silver Dagger" focuses on the harsh realities of modern adolescence and the ever present threat of bullying, all to common to younger women. The poem vividly captures a scene of the subject contemplating suicide, though it leaves the reader with a dark, yet hopeful note. Suicide is one of the leading causes of death among teens, and the internet has allowed bullying to present itself in a different way that it has more traditionally taken. It saddens me to think that this harsh reality is a part of our society and often goes unpunished.

The poem offers a glimpse into the mind of an adolescent woman who can take no more. In many ways, the subject appears to have already died metaphorically. In combination with all of the self esteem challenges young women face due to the cruel vision of physical perfection, Katie masterfully captures the very moment when the situation becomes a life and death decision for the subject. Katie captures the fear of the moment through her choice of the instrument of death almost as if bullying has murdered the victim.

When tasked with providing an analysis of "Silver Dagger", I was initially apprehensive. Suicide is a taboo subject to discuss. However, I'm glad the poem was written. Suicide needs to become a public conversation, and painting the true picture of suicide gives the message of the poem more weight when communicating one of the harsh realities of modern adolescence.

"A Blooming Friendship" focuses on the impact of mental health and addiction on the lives of others. In the case of this poem, I am writing of an experience when I lost someone close to me. The scenery I have created demonstrates that, before the tragic turn of events, I see beauty in the world and am looking forward to the events that will unfold. The reader at this point is likely to expect a happy ending. I wrote the poem with this in mind. The idea was to to show how quickly a person's life can change when someone they know begins to turn to drugs to cope with depression.

The reader learns in the lines, "we would talk of swimming in the ocean.....respite from the prison of our troubled minds" that both myself and my friend have serious obstacles to overcome. In "Silver Dagger", the subject does not end her life in that moment, but it is possible that she may eventually do so. In "A Blooming Friendship", I lose my friend to depression and addiction. The last three lines of the poem powerfully depict the overwhelming sadness of losing someone to suicide.

The poem I have written in this pair is a piece I will most likely hold on to for the rest of my life. This book is the third collection I've put together where the poem makes an appearance. When I read the poem, I'm able to think of the good times and hard times we experienced together while being reminded of her being in my life. She is one of the best friends I've ever had. When reading "Silver Dagger" and "A Blooming Friendship, think of the connection between the personal experience of depression and the effect of losing someone to suicide on those who care about them.

Silver Dagger
Written by Kaitlin Shearer

She is pain, nobody can see it,

Bleeding from the inside, crying out for help,

Nobody cares, nobody notices,

This is what she tells herself, lying on her bathroom floor,

Her hand shaking, pondering the thought of death

She will either send the dagger plunging into her frozen body,

Or live a long life, hating every moment of it

Tears roll down her rosy cheeks,

She holds the dagger higher,

Sharp blade gently aligned with her heart,

Would she do it? Time will tell

A Blooming Friendship
Written by David Stant

A splendid spring day,

Beautiful flowers budding,

People strolling and shopping on downtown streets

I was approaching the world openly,

Hoping to find peace of mind;

I saw her, among her friends,

Reflecting a light, cool breeze,

Unbeknownst I had met my best friend

She taught me the most of love,

Than I had learned in my previous thirty years;

We would talk of swimming in the ocean,

Years of hope washed away by crashing waves,

A respite from the prison of our troubled minds;

Opiates stole from me her love,

The beautiful flowers now wilted,

I've seen hate grow,

And I return as if I never met her